Contents

54

APPETIZERS

BLT Dip

PREP: 15 min. **TOTAL:** 15 min.

- 1 pkg. (8 oz.) **PHILADELPHIA** Cream Cheese, softened
- ¾ cup shredded or chopped romaine lettuce
- 2 plum tomatoes, seeded, chopped
- 4 slices **OSCAR MAYER** Bacon, crisply cooked, drained and crumbled

SPREAD cream cheese onto bottom of 9-inch pie plate.

TOP with lettuce and tomatoes; sprinkle with bacon.

SERVE with **WHEAT THINS** Snack Crackers or assorted cut-up fresh vegetables.

Makes 2 cups or 16 servings, 2 Tbsp. each.

Make Ahead: Dip can be stored, tightly covered, in refrigerator up to 1 hour before serving.

How to Soften Cream Cheese: Place completely unwrapped package of cream cheese in microwaveable 9-inch pie plate. Microwave on HIGH 15 sec. or just until softened. Spread onto bottom of pie plate, then continue as directed.

Spinach-Stuffed Mushrooms

PREP: 15 min. **TOTAL:** 35 min.

1	pkg. (6 oz.) **STOVE TOP** Stuffing Mix for Chicken
1½	cups hot water
40	fresh mushrooms (2 lb.)
2	Tbsp. butter
2	cloves garlic, minced
1	pkg. (10 oz.) frozen chopped spinach, thawed, well drained
1	cup **KRAFT** Shredded Low-Moisture Part-Skim Mozzarella Cheese
1	cup **KRAFT** Grated Parmesan Cheese

HEAT oven to 400°F. Mix stuffing mix and hot water. Remove stems from mushrooms; chop stems. Melt butter in skillet on medium heat. Add chopped stems and garlic; cook and stir until tender. Stir into prepared stuffing along with spinach and cheeses.

SPOON into mushrooms; place in shallow baking pan.

BAKE 20 min. or until filling is heated through.

Makes 40 servings, 1 mushroom each.

Leftover Stuffing: Since mushrooms vary in size, you may have some leftover stuffing mixture. If so, heat it and serve as a side dish with chicken.

Cheesy Spinach and Artichoke Dip

PREP: 10 min. **TOTAL:** 30 min.

- **1 can (14 oz.) artichoke hearts, drained, finely chopped**
- **1 pkg. (10 oz.) frozen chopped spinach, thawed, drained**
- **¾ cup KRAFT Grated Parmesan Cheese**
- **¾ cup KRAFT Light Mayonnaise**
- **½ cup KRAFT 2% Milk Shredded Mozzarella Cheese**
- **½ tsp. garlic powder**

HEAT oven to 350°F. Mix all ingredients; spoon into quiche dish or pie plate.

BAKE 20 min. or until heated through.

SERVE with **TRISCUIT** Reduced Fat Crackers and assorted cut-up fresh vegetables.

Makes 2¾ cups or 22 servings, 2 Tbsp. each.

Awesome Spinach and Mushroom Dip:
Substitute 1 cup chopped fresh mushrooms for the artichokes.

Layered Italian Dip

PREP: 10 min. **TOTAL:** 25 min.

- **1 pkg. (8 oz.) PHILADELPHIA** Cream Cheese, softened
- **¼ cup KRAFT** Grated Parmesan Cheese
- **⅓ cup pesto**
- **½ cup roasted red peppers, drained, chopped**
- **1 cup KRAFT** Shredded Mozzarella Cheese

HEAT oven to 350°F. Mix cream cheese and Parmesan cheese; spread into pie plate.

TOP with remaining ingredients.

BAKE 15 min. or until heated through. Serve with **NABISCO** Crackers.

Makes 2 cups or 16 servings, 2 Tbsp. each.

Variation: Prepare using **PHILADELPHIA** Neufchâtel Cheese, and **KRAFT** 2% Milk Shredded Mozzarella Cheese.

Special Extra: Garnish with sliced black olives and fresh basil.

Hot Crab Dip

PREP: 15 min. **TOTAL:** 45 min.

- **2 pkg. (8 oz. each) PHILADELPHIA** Cream Cheese, softened
- **2 cans (6 oz. each) crabmeat, drained, flaked**
- **½ cup KRAFT Shredded Parmesan Cheese**
- **2 green onions, sliced**
- **2 Tbsp. dry white wine**
- **1 Tbsp. KRAFT Horseradish Sauce**
- **1 tsp. hot pepper sauce**

HEAT oven to 350°F. Beat all ingredients with mixer until blended.

SPOON into pie plate.

BAKE 25 to 30 min. or until lightly browned. Serve with **NABISCO** Crackers and cut up fresh vegetables.

Makes 3½ cups or 28 servings, 2 Tbsp. each.

Keeping It Safe: Even canned crabmeat can contain tiny pieces of shell, so use your just-washed fingers to pick over the crabmeat before adding to a recipe.

Substitute: Prepare using **PHILADELPHIA** Neufchâtel Cheese.

Bacon Appetizer Crescents

PREP: 30 min. **TOTAL:** 45 min.

- 1 pkg. (8 oz.) **PHILADELPHIA** Cream Cheese, softened
- 8 slices **OSCAR MAYER** Bacon, crisply cooked, crumbled
- ⅓ cup **KRAFT** Grated Parmesan Cheese
- ¼ cup finely chopped onions
- 2 Tbsp. chopped fresh parsley
- 1 Tbsp. milk
- 2 cans (8 oz. each) refrigerated crescent dinner rolls

HEAT oven to 375°F. Mix all ingredients except dough.

SEPARATE each can of dough into 4 rectangles; firmly press perforations together to seal. Spread each rectangle with ¼ of cream cheese mixture. Cut each rectangle into 12 wedges; roll up, starting at short ends. Place, seam-sides down, on greased baking sheet.

BAKE 12 to 15 min. or until golden brown.

Makes 8 doz. or 24 servings, 4 crescents each.

Substitute: Prepare using **PHILADELPHIA** Neufchâtel Cheese.

Special Extra: Sprinkle lightly with poppy seeds before baking.

SIDE DISHES

KRAFT Golden Parmesan Potatoes

PREP: 10 min. **TOTAL:** 55 min.

- 2 lb. new potatoes, quartered
- ¼ cup olive oil
- 1½ tsp. Italian seasoning
- 2 cloves garlic, minced
- ⅓ cup **KRAFT** Grated Parmesan Cheese

HEAT oven to 400°F. Toss potatoes with oil, seasoning and garlic. Add cheese; mix lightly.

SPREAD into 15×10×1-inch baking pan.

BAKE 45 min. or until potatoes are tender.

Makes 6 servings.

Substitute: Prepare using **KRAFT** Grated Parmesan and Romano Cheese.

Zesty Grilled Veggies

PREP: 10 min. **TOTAL:** 20 min.

- **4** zucchini (1½ lb.), cut diagonally into ½-inch-thick slices
- **3** each: red and yellow bell peppers (1¾ lb.), cut into ½-inch-wide strips
- **¼** cup **KRAFT** Zesty Italian Dressing
- **¼** cup **KRAFT** Grated Parmesan Cheese

HEAT grill to medium. Place vegetables in grill basket.

GRILL 10 min. or until crisp-tender, turning occasionally. Place in large bowl.

ADD dressing; toss to coat. Sprinkle with cheese.

Makes 8 servings.

Cooking Know-How: Don't have a grill basket? Cover grill grate with large sheet of heavy-duty foil before heating as directed. Spread vegetables onto foil. Grill as directed, stirring occasionally.

How to Buy Peppers: Look for peppers with very bright colors and a firm thick flesh. Refrigerate unwashed peppers in a plastic bag for up to 2 weeks.

Cheesy Smashed Potatoes

PREP: 15 min. **TOTAL:** 35 min.

- 1 **lb. red potatoes (about 3 small), cut into chunks**
- 1 **cup bite-size cauliflower florets**
- ¼ **cup BREAKSTONE'S Reduced Fat or KNUDSEN Light Sour Cream**
- 1 **cup KRAFT 2% Milk Shredded Sharp Cheddar Cheese**

COOK vegetables in boiling water 20 min. or until tender. Drain; return to pan.

ADD sour cream; mash until light and fluffy. Stir in cheese.

Makes 6 servings, ½ cup each.

Substitute: Substitute 1 cup frozen cauliflower florets for the fresh cauliflower.

Use Your Microwave: Place potatoes and cauliflower in large microwaveable bowl; add water to cover. Cover with waxed paper. Microwave on HIGH 20 min. or until vegetables are very tender. Continue as directed.

Mashed Potato Layer Bake

PREP: 25 min. **TOTAL:** 45 min.

- 4 large white potatoes, peeled, chopped and cooked
- 2 large sweet potatoes, peeled, chopped and cooked
- 1 tub (8 oz.) **PHILADELPHIA** Chive & Onion Cream Cheese Spread, divided
- ½ cup **BREAKSTONE'S** or **KNUDSEN** Sour Cream, divided
- ¼ tsp. each: salt and black pepper
- ¼ cup **KRAFT** Shredded Parmesan Cheese, divided
- ¼ cup **KRAFT** Shredded Cheddar Cheese, divided

HEAT oven to 375°F. Place potatoes in separate bowls. Add ½ each of the cream cheese spread and sour cream to each bowl; season with salt and pepper. Mash until creamy.

STIR ½ the Parmesan cheese into white potatoes. Stir half of the Cheddar cheese into sweet potatoes. Alternately layer ½ each of the white potato and sweet potato mixtures in 2-qt. casserole dish. Repeat layers.

BAKE 15 min. Sprinkle with remaining cheeses; bake 5 min. or until melted.

Makes 14 servings, ½ cup each.

Make Ahead: Assemble casserole as directed but do not add the cheese topping. Refrigerate casserole and cheese topping separately up to 3 days. When ready to serve, bake casserole as directed, increasing baking time as needed until casserole is heated through. Top with remaining cheeses and continue as directed.

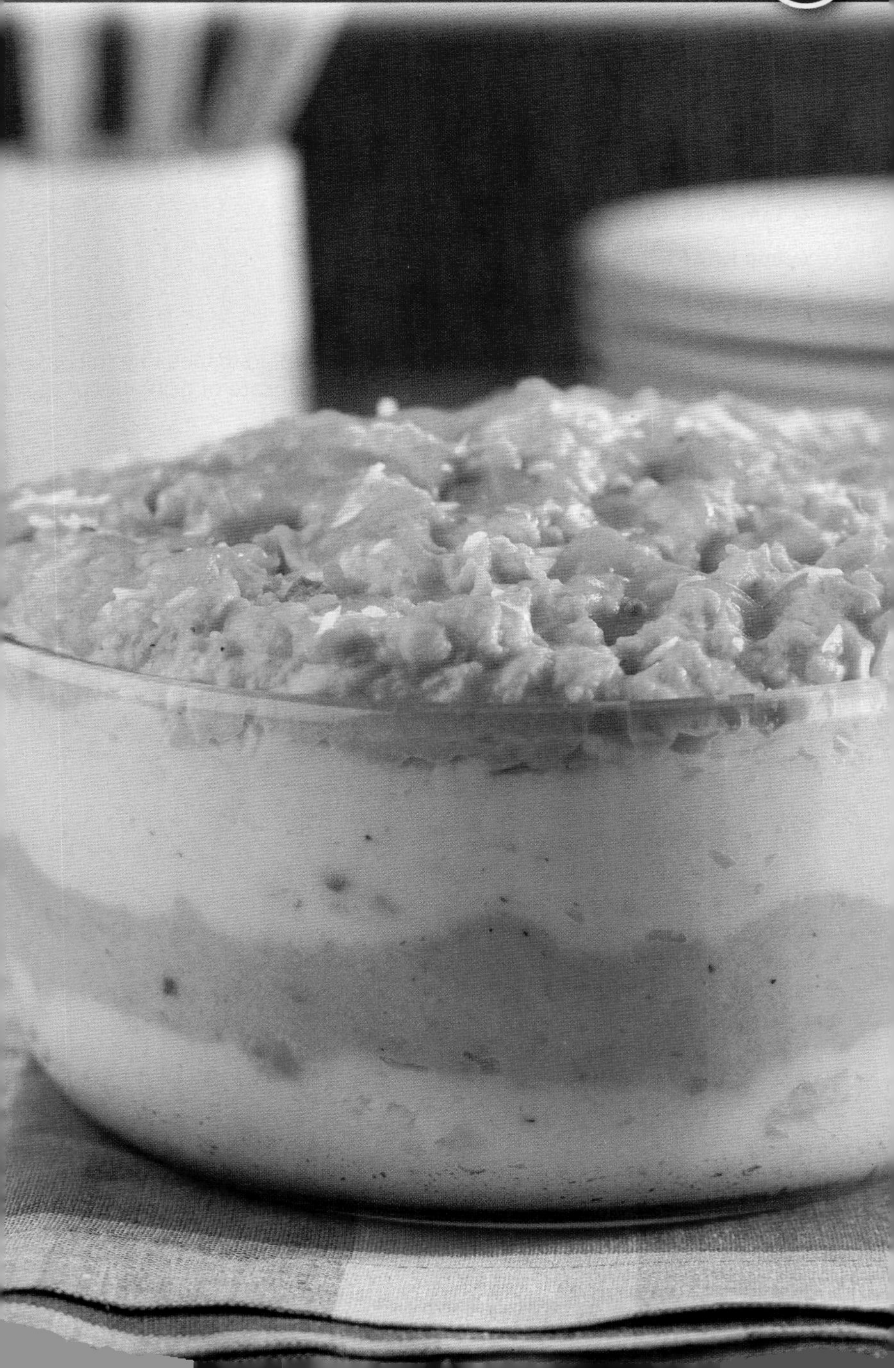

Easy "Baked" Tomatoes

PREP: 5 min. **TOTAL:** 20 min.

- **4** tomatoes, cut in half
- ¼ cup **KRAFT** Balsamic Vinaigrette Dressing
- ¼ cup **KRAFT** Grated Parmesan Cheese

HEAT grill to medium. Place tomatoes, cut-sides up, in disposable foil pan. Top with dressing and cheese. Place pan on grate of grill; close lid.

GRILL 15 min. or until tomatoes are soft and cheese is lightly browned.

Makes 4 servings.

How to Use Your Oven: Heat oven to 350°F. Place tomato halves, cut-sides up, in a 13×9-inch baking dish. Top with dressing and cheese as directed. Bake 15 to 20 min. or until tomatoes are soft and cheese is lightly browned.

Special Extra: Sprinkle with 1 Tbsp. chopped fresh basil or parsley before grilling as directed.

Substitute: For variety, prepare with **KRAFT** Sun-Dried Tomato Dressing.

Cheesy Harvest Vegetables

PREP: 35 min. **TOTAL:** 1 hour 5 min.

- **2 lb. mixed fall vegetables (butternut squash, sweet potatoes, turnips, parsnips and carrots), peeled, cut into 1-inch cubes**
- **3 cups milk**
- **1 pkg. (8 oz.) PHILADELPHIA Cream Cheese, cubed**
- **1 cup KRAFT Shredded Parmesan Cheese**
- **⅛ tsp. ground nutmeg**
- **8 RITZ Crackers, crushed**

HEAT oven to 350°F. Bring vegetables and milk to boil in large saucepan on medium-high heat. Reduce heat to medium-low; simmer 20 min. or until vegetables are tender, stirring occasionally. Add cream cheese; cook until melted, stirring frequently. Stir in Parmesan cheese and nutmeg.

SPOON into greased 2-qt. casserole dish; sprinkle with crumbs.

BAKE 30 min. or until heated through.

Makes 10 servings, about ¾ cup each.

Size-Wise: Enjoy a serving of this cheesy vegetable side dish at your next special occasion.

Make Ahead: Assemble recipe as directed except do not add crumb topping. Refrigerate up to 24 hours. When ready to serve, sprinkle with the cracker crumbs. Bake as directed, increasing the baking time to 40 min. or until heated through.

Easy Vegetable Toss

PREP: 15 min. **TOTAL:** 3 hours 15 min. (incl. refrigerating)

- 1 lb. broccoli florets
- 1 lb. cauliflower florets
- ½ lb. green beans
- 1 large red bell pepper, cut into strips
- ½ cup **KRAFT** Zesty Italian Dressing
- ⅓ cup **KRAFT** Shredded Parmesan Cheese

COOK broccoli, cauliflower and beans in boiling water 3 to 5 min. or just until crisp-tender. (Do not overcook.) Drain. Immediately rinse with very cold water; drain again. Place in large bowl.

STIR in peppers. Refrigerate several hours or until chilled.

ADD dressing and cheese just before serving; mix lightly.

Makes 16 servings, ¾ cup each.

Serve it Hot: For a change of pace, serve hot. Cook vegetables as directed; drain. Add remaining ingredients; mix lightly. Serve immediately.

Variation: Prepare as directed, using **KRAFT** Sun-Dried Tomato Dressing and **KRAFT** Grated Parmesan Cheese.

CASEROLES

Creamy Chicken and Pasta Casserole

PREP: 15 min. **TOTAL:** 40 min.

- ¾ cup each: chopped celery, red onions and red peppers
- 1 pkg. (8 oz.) **PHILADELPHIA** Cream Cheese, cubed
- 2 cups milk
- ¼ tsp. garlic salt
- 4 cups cooked rotini pasta
- 3 cups chopped cooked chicken breasts
- ½ cup **KRAFT** Grated Parmesan Cheese, divided

HEAT oven to 350°F. Heat large nonstick skillet sprayed with cooking spray on medium heat. Add vegetables; cook and stir 3 min. or until crisp-tender. Add cream cheese, milk and garlic salt; cook on low heat 3 to 5 min. or until cream cheese is melted, stirring frequently.

ADD pasta, chicken and ¼ cup Parmesan cheese; spoon into 2½-qt. casserole dish.

BAKE 20 to 25 min. or until heated through. Sprinkle with remaining Parmesan cheese.

Makes 6 servings.

Serving Suggestion: Serve with a mixed green salad tossed with your favorite **KRAFT** Dressing.

Variation: Prepare using **PHILADELPHIA** Neufchâtel Cheese, fat-free milk and whole wheat rotini pasta.

Easy Baked Manicotti

PREP: 25 min. **TOTAL:** 1 hour 5 min.

- 2 cups spaghetti sauce, divided
- 1 egg, beaten
- 1¾ cups **POLLY-O** Original Ricotta Cheese
- 1½ cups **KRAFT** Shredded Mozzarella Cheese
- ½ cup **KRAFT** Grated Parmesan Cheese
- ¼ cup pesto
- 12 manicotti shells, cooked, rinsed in cold water

HEAT oven to 350°F. Spread ¾ cup sauce onto bottom of 13×9-inch baking dish. Mix egg, cheeses and pesto; spoon into resealable plastic bag. Cut small hole in bottom corner of bag; use to squeeze cheese mixture into both ends of each shell.

PLACE in dish; top with remaining spaghetti sauce. Cover with foil.

BAKE 40 min. or until heated through.

Makes 6 servings, 2 manicotti each.

Size-Wise: Enjoy your favorite foods on occasion, but keep portion size in mind. This recipe makes enough to serve 6.

Make Ahead: Cook manicotti shells up to 1 day ahead. Place on greased tray, cover with plastic wrap and refrigerate until ready to fill.

Substitute: Substitute **BREAKSTONE'S** or **KNUDSEN** Cottage Cheese for the ricotta cheese and/or **KRAFT** Grated Romano Cheese for the Parmesan cheese.

One-Pan Chicken and Potato Bake

PREP: 10 min. **TOTAL:** 1 hour 10 min.

4 bone-in chicken pieces (1½ lb.)

1½ lb. potatoes (about 3), cut into thin wedges

¼ cup **KRAFT** Zesty Italian Dressing

¼ cup **KRAFT** Grated Parmesan Cheese

1 tsp. Italian seasoning

HEAT oven to 400°F. Place chicken and potatoes in 13×9-inch baking dish.

TOP with dressing, cheese and seasoning; cover with foil.

BAKE 1 hour or until chicken is cooked through (165°F), removing foil after 30 min.

Makes 4 servings.

Serving Suggestion: Serve a tossed green salad tossed with your favorite **KRAFT** Dressing.

Storage Tips for Potatoes: The best way to store potatoes is in a ventilated container in a dry dark place. Avoid storing potatoes with onions since the potatoes readily absorb odors.

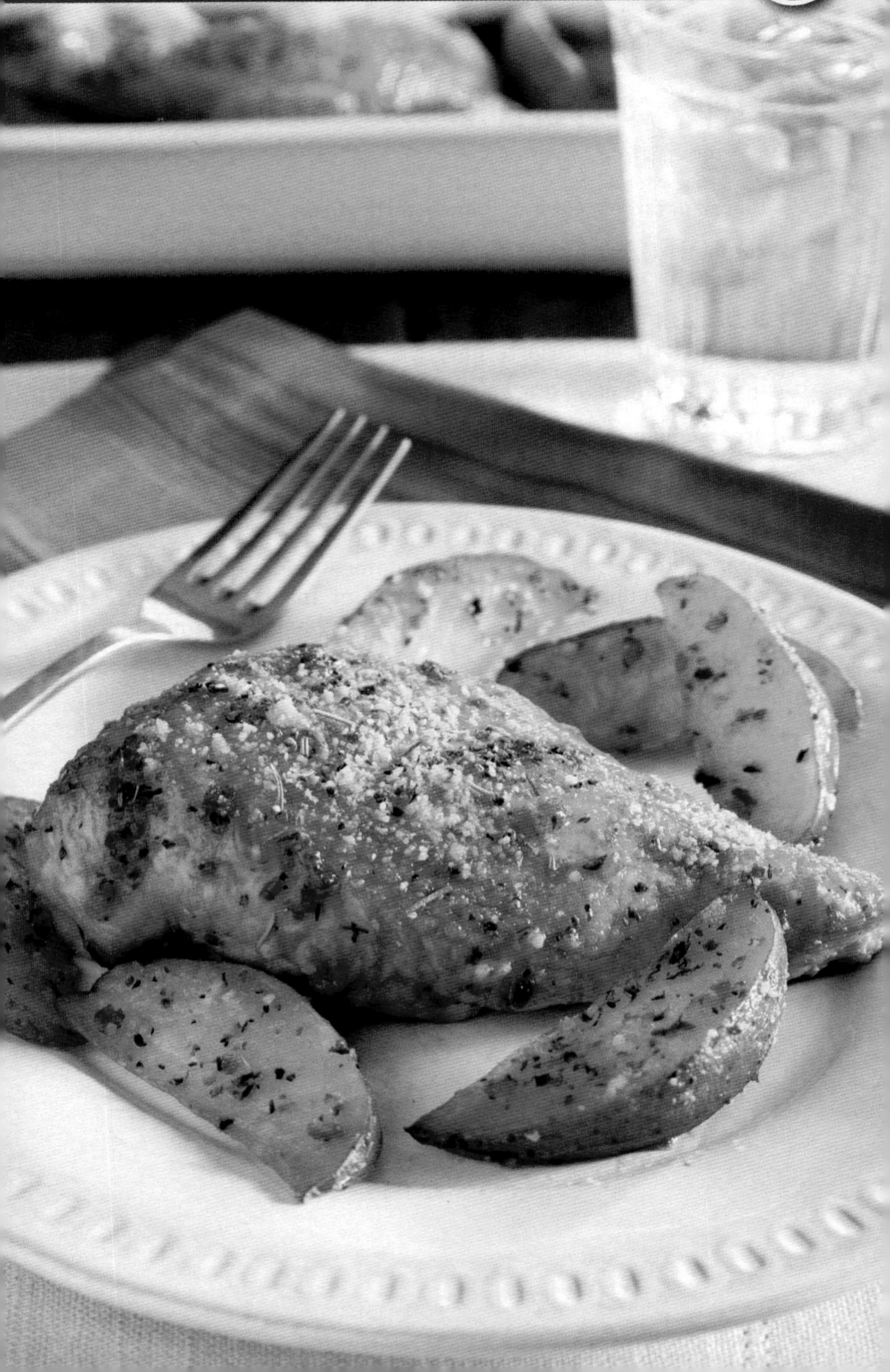

New-Look Scalloped Potatoes and Ham

PREP: 30 min. **TOTAL:** 1 hour

- 4½ lb. red potatoes, cut into ¼-inch-thick slices
- 1 container (16 oz.) **BREAKSTONE'S FREE** or **KNUDSEN FREE** Fat Free Sour Cream
- ¾ lb. (12 oz.) **VELVEETA** 2% Milk Pasteurized Prepared Cheese Product, cut into ½-inch cubes
- ½ lb. (½ of 1-lb. pkg.) **OSCAR MAYER** Smoked Ham, chopped
- 4 green onions, sliced
- ¼ cup **KRAFT** Grated Parmesan Cheese

HEAT oven to 350°F. Cook potatoes in boiling water in covered large saucepan 10 to 12 min. or just until potatoes are tender; drain. Place ¾ of potatoes in large bowl. Add sour cream; mash until smooth. Stir in **VELVEETA**, ham and onions. Add remaining potatoes; mix lightly.

SPOON into 13×9-inch baking dish sprayed with cooking spray; sprinkle with Parmesan cheese.

BAKE 30 min. or until heated through.

Makes 16 servings, about 1 cup each.

Purchasing Potatoes: Look for firm, smooth, well-shaped potatoes that are free of wrinkles, cracks and blemishes. Avoid any with green-tinged skins or sprouting "eyes" or buds.

Size-Wise: Enjoy your favorite foods on occasion, but keep portion size in mind.

Easy Italian Pasta Bake

PREP: 20 min. **TOTAL:** 40 min.

- **1 lb. extra lean ground beef**
- **3 cups whole wheat penne pasta, cooked, drained**
- **1 jar (26 oz.) spaghetti sauce**
- **⅓ cup KRAFT Grated Parmesan Cheese, divided**
- **1½ cups KRAFT 2% Milk Shredded Mozzarella Cheese**

HEAT oven to 375°F. Brown meat in large skillet; drain. Stir in pasta, sauce and ½ the Parmesan cheese.

SPOON into 13×9-inch baking dish; top with remaining cheeses.

BAKE 20 min. or until heated through.

Makes 6 servings, 1⅓ cups each.

Substitute: Substitute regular penne pasta for the whole wheat penne pasta.

Special Extra: Brown meat with 1 tsp. Italian seasoning and 3 cloves garlic, minced.

Serving Suggestion: Serve with mixed green salad tossed with your favorite **KRAFT** Dressing.

Bruschetta Chicken Bake

PREP: 10 min. **TOTAL:** 40 min.

- 1 can (14½ oz.) diced tomatoes, undrained
- 1 pkg. (6 oz.) **STOVE TOP** Stuffing Mix for Chicken
- ½ cup water
- 2 cloves garlic, minced
- 1½ lb. boneless, skinless chicken breasts, cut into bite-size pieces
- 1 tsp. dried basil leaves
- 1 cup **KRAFT** Shredded Low-Moisture Part-Skim Mozzarella Cheese

HEAT oven to 400°F. Stir tomatoes, stuffing mix, water and garlic just until stuffing mix is moistened.

PLACE chicken in 13×9-inch baking dish; sprinkle with basil. Top with cheese and stuffing mixture.

BAKE 30 min. or until chicken is cooked through.

Makes 6 servings, 1 cup each.

Serving Suggestion: Serve with cooked green beans and a bagged green salad tossed with your favorite **KRAFT** Light Dressing.

Turkey-Parmesan Casserole

PREP: 20 min. **TOTAL:** 50 min.

- 8 oz. spaghetti, broken in half, uncooked
- 1 can (10¾ oz.) condensed cream of mushroom soup
- ¾ cup **BREAKSTONE'S** or **KNUDSEN** Sour Cream
- ¼ cup milk
- ⅓ cup **KRAFT** Grated Parmesan Cheese
- ¼ tsp. black pepper
- 3 cups frozen broccoli florets, thawed
- 2 cups chopped cooked turkey

HEAT oven to 350°F. Cook spaghetti as directed on package; drain.

MIX soup, sour cream, milk, Parmesan cheese and pepper in large bowl. Add spaghetti, broccoli and turkey; mix lightly. Spoon into 2-qt. casserole dish.

BAKE 25 to 30 min. or until heated through.

Makes: 6 servings, 1⅓ cups each.

Substitute: Substitute frozen cut green beans or peas for broccoli.

Substitute: Prepare using **KRAFT** Grated Parmesan and Romano Cheese.

Taco Bake

PREP: 15 min. **TOTAL:** 35 min.

- 1 pkg. (14 oz.) **KRAFT** Deluxe Macaroni & Cheese Dinner
- 1 lb. ground beef
- 1 pkg. **TACO BELL® HOME ORIGINALS®** Taco Seasoning Mix
- ¾ cup **BREAKSTONE'S** or **KNUDSEN** Sour Cream
- 1½ cups **KRAFT** Shredded Cheddar Cheese
- 1 cup **TACO BELL® HOME ORIGINALS®** Thick 'N Chunky Salsa

HEAT oven to 400°F. Prepare Dinner as directed on package. While Macaroni is cooking, cook meat with taco seasoning mix as directed on package.

STIR sour cream into prepared Dinner; spoon ½ into 8-inch square baking dish. Top with layers of meat mixture, 1 cup Cheddar cheese and remaining Dinner mixture; cover with foil.

BAKE 15 min. Top with salsa and remaining Cheddar. Bake, uncovered, 5 min. or until Cheddar is melted.

Makes 6 servings, 1 cup each.

Variation: Prepare using **BREAKSTONE'S** Reduced Fat or **KNUDSEN** Light Sour Cream, and **KRAFT** 2% Milk Shredded Cheddar Cheese.

Serving Suggestion: Serve with your favorite hot cooked vegetable, such as broccoli.

TACO BELL® and HOME ORIGINALS® are trademarks owned and licensed by Taco Bell Corp.

Cheesy Tuna Noodle Casserole

PREP: 20 min. **TOTAL:** 59 min.

- 1 bag (16 oz.) frozen vegetable blend (broccoli, carrots, cauliflower)
- 1 pkg. (14 oz.) **KRAFT** Deluxe Macaroni & Cheese Dinner Made With 2% Milk Cheese
- ¾ cup fat-free milk
- ¼ cup **KRAFT** Light Zesty Italian Dressing
- 1 can (12 oz.) white tuna in water, drained, flaked
- 1 cup **KRAFT** 2% Milk Shredded Sharp Cheddar Cheese, divided

HEAT oven to 375°F. Place vegetables in colander in sink. Cook Macaroni as directed on package. Pour over vegetables in colander to drain macaroni and quickly thaw vegetables.

RETURN macaroni and vegetables to saucepan. Stir in Cheese Sauce, milk and dressing. Add tuna and ½ cup Cheddar cheese; mix well. Spoon into 2-qt. casserole dish; cover with foil.

BAKE 35 min. or until heated through. Uncover; top with remaining Cheddar cheese. Bake 3 to 4 min. or until cheese is melted.

Makes 5 servings, about 1½ cups each.

Substitute: Substitute 1 lb. extra lean ground beef, cooked and drained, for the tuna.

Make Ahead: Assemble casserole as directed; cover. Refrigerate up to 24 hours. When ready to serve, bake, covered, at 375°F for 40 to 45 min. or until heated through. Remove from oven; uncover. Sprinkle with remaining Cheddar cheese. Let stand 5 min. or until cheese is melted.

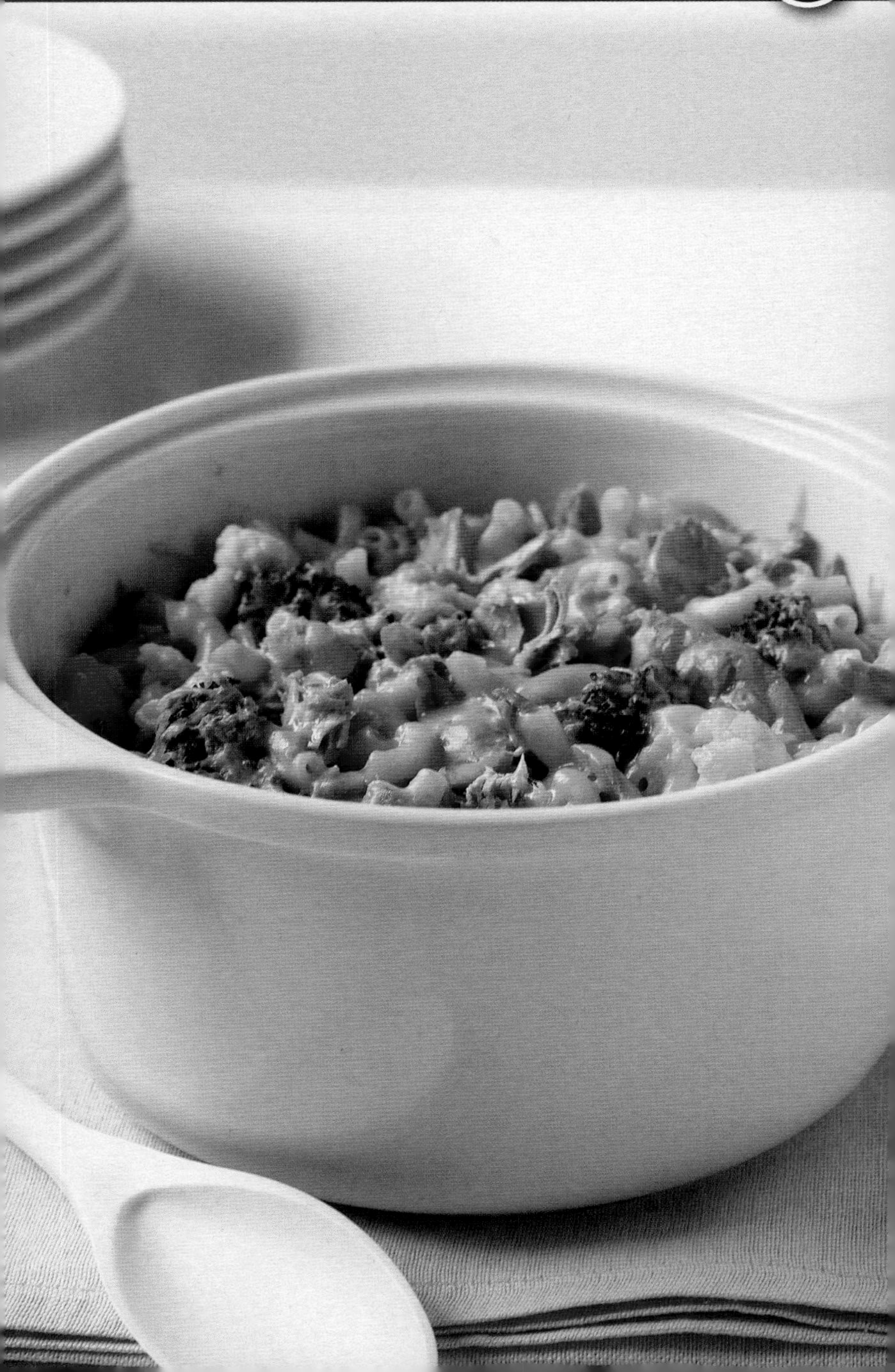

PASTA

Garden-Fresh Pasta Salad

PREP: 20 min. **TOTAL:** 1 hour 30 min. (incl. refrigerating)

- 1 pkg. (1 lb.) farfalle (bow-tie pasta), uncooked
- 2 cups broccoli florets
- 1 small red onion, thinly sliced
- 1 red bell pepper, chopped
- 1 cup halved cherry tomatoes
- 1 bottle (8 oz.) **KRAFT** Sun-Dried Tomato Dressing
- ½ cup **KRAFT** Grated Parmesan Cheese

COOK pasta as directed on package, adding broccoli for the last 3 min. Drain; rinse under cold water. Drain well; place in large bowl.

ADD onions, peppers and tomatoes; mix lightly. Toss with dressing.

REFRIGERATE 1 hour. Stir before serving; sprinkle with cheese.

Makes 14 servings, ¾ cup each.

Substitute: Substitute 1-inch asparagus pieces for the broccoli.

Substitute: Prepare using **KRAFT** Shredded Parmesan Cheese; or **KRAFT** Shredded Parmesan, Romano and Asiago Cheese.

Simply Lasagna

PREP: 20 min. **TOTAL:** 1 hour 20 min.

1 **lb. ground beef**

1 **egg, beaten**

2½ **cups KRAFT Shredded Low-Moisture Part-Skim Mozzarella Cheese, divided**

1 **container (15 oz.) POLLY-O Natural Part Skim Ricotta Cheese**

½ **cup KRAFT Grated Parmesan Cheese, divided**

¼ **cup chopped fresh parsley**

1 **jar (26 oz.) spaghetti sauce**

1 **cup water**

12 **lasagna noodles, uncooked**

HEAT oven to 350°F. Brown meat in large skillet. Meanwhile, mix egg, 1¼ cups mozzarella cheese, ricotta cheese, ¼ cup Parmesan cheese and parsley.

DRAIN meat; return to skillet. Stir in sauce. Add water to empty sauce jar; cover with lid and shake well. Stir into meat. Spread 1 cup sauce onto bottom of 13×9-inch baking dish; top with layers of 3 noodles, ⅓ ricotta cheese mixture and 1 cup sauce. Repeat layers twice. Top with remaining noodles, sauce and cheeses. Cover with greased foil.

BAKE 45 min. Remove foil; bake 15 min. or until heated through. Let stand 15 min.

Makes 12 servings.

Size-Wise: Since this comfort-food classic serves 12, it's a perfect dish to serve at your next gathering.

Easy Cleanup: Greasing the foil before using to cover the lasagna will help prevent the cheese from sticking to it.

Shortcut: Adding water to the sauce helps cook traditional noodles during baking, so you don't have to cook them beforehand. This saves you 15 to 20 min. of prep time.

Fettuccine Alfredo

PREP: 5 min. **TOTAL:** 20 min.

- 4 oz. (½ of 8-oz. pkg.) **PHILADELPHIA** Cream Cheese, cubed
- ½ cup **KRAFT** Grated Parmesan Cheese
- ¾ cup milk
- ¼ cup (½ stick) butter or margarine
- ¼ tsp. white pepper
- ⅛ tsp. garlic powder
- 8 oz. fettuccine, cooked, drained
- ⅛ tsp. ground nutmeg

PLACE cream cheese, Parmesan cheese, milk, butter, white pepper and garlic powder in medium saucepan; cook and stir on low heat until cream cheese is melted.

TOSS with hot fettuccine. Sprinkle with nutmeg.

Makes 4 servings, about 1 cup each.

Serving Suggestion: Try serving with Italian bread and a mixed green salad tossed with your favorite **KRAFT** Dressing, such as Balsamic Vinaigrette.

Special Extra: Prepare as directed, heating 1 pkg. (6 oz.) **OSCAR MAYER** Grilled or Italian Style Chicken Breast Strips with the sauce before tossing with pasta.

Substitute: Prepare using **PHILADELPHIA** Neufchâtel Cheese.

Low-Fat Zesty Shrimp and Pasta

PREP: 10 min. **TOTAL:** 25 min.

- ½ **lb. linguine, uncooked**
- ¾ **cup prepared GOOD SEASONS Zesty Italian Salad Dressing & Recipe Mix for Fat Free Dressing, divided**
- 2 **cups sliced fresh mushrooms**
- 1 **small onion, thinly sliced**
- 1 **can (14 oz.) artichoke hearts, drained, quartered**
- 1 **lb. uncooked deveined peeled large shrimp**
- 1 **Tbsp. chopped fresh parsley**
- ¼ **cup KRAFT Grated Parmesan Cheese**

COOK pasta in large saucepan as directed on package.

MEANWHILE, heat ½ cup dressing in large skillet on medium heat. Stir in mushrooms, onions and artichokes; cook and stir 3 min. or until onions are crisp-tender. Add shrimp and parsley; stir. Cook 2 min. or until shrimp turn pink, stirring occasionally.

DRAIN pasta; return to pan. Toss with shrimp mixture and remaining dressing; sprinkle with cheese.

Makes 6 servings.

Substitute: Prepare substituting scallops for the shrimp and 1 large red bell pepper, chopped, for the artichoke hearts.

Substitute: Prepare using **KRAFT** Light House Italian Dressing.

Better-than-Ever Cheesy Meat Lasagna

PREP: 30 min. **TOTAL:** 1 hour 10 min.

- ¾ **lb. extra lean ground beef**
- 3 **cloves garlic, minced**
- 1½ **tsp. dried oregano leaves**
- 1 **jar (26 oz.) spaghetti sauce**
- 1 **large tomato, chopped**
- 1 **egg, beaten**
- 1 **container (16 oz.) BREAKSTONE'S or KNUDSEN Low Fat Cottage Cheese**
- ¼ **cup KRAFT Grated Parmesan Cheese**
- 9 **lasagna noodles, cooked, drained**
- 2 **cups KRAFT 2% Milk Shredded Mozzarella Cheese, divided**

HEAT oven to 375°F. Brown meat with garlic and oregano in medium saucepan. Stir in spaghetti sauce; simmer 5 min., stirring occasionally. Remove from heat; stir in tomatoes.

MIX egg, cottage cheese and Parmesan cheese; spread ½ cup onto bottom of 13×9-inch baking dish. Top with layers of 3 noodles, 1 cup cottage cheese mixture, ½ cup mozzarella cheese and 1 cup of the remaining spaghetti sauce mixture. Repeat layers. Top with remaining noodles and spaghetti sauce mixture. Cover with foil.

BAKE 30 min. or until heated through. Top with remaining cheese. Bake, uncovered, 5 min. or until cheese is melted. Let stand 5 min.

Makes 9 servings.

Make Ahead: Assemble lasagna as directed; cover. Refrigerate up to 24 hours. When ready to serve, bake, covered, at 375°F for 40 min. or until heated through.

Cheesy Stuffed Shells

PREP: 30 min. **TOTAL:** 57 min.

- 1 jar (26 oz.) spaghetti sauce
- 1 large tomato, chopped
- 1 container (16 oz.) **BREAKSTONE'S** or **KNUDSEN** Low Fat Cottage Cheese
- 1 pkg. (10 oz.) frozen chopped spinach, thawed, well drained
- 1 cup **KRAFT** 2% Milk Shredded Mozzarella Cheese, divided
- ¼ cup **KRAFT** Grated Parmesan Cheese
- 1 tsp. Italian seasoning
- 20 jumbo pasta shells, cooked, drained

HEAT oven to 400°F. Mix sauce and tomatoes; spoon ½ into 13×9-inch baking dish.

MIX cottage cheese, spinach, ½ cup mozzarella cheese, Parmesan cheese and seasoning; spoon into shells. Place in dish; top with remaining sauce mixture. Cover with foil.

BAKE 25 min. or until heated through. Top with remaining cheese. Bake, uncovered, 2 min. or until cheese is melted.

Makes 5 servings, 4 stuffed shells each.

Make it Easy: To help prevent the cheese from sticking to the foil, spray it with cooking spray before using to cover the unbaked shells.

Make Ahead: Assemble recipe as directed; cover. Refrigerate up to 24 hours. When ready to serve, bake, covered, at 400°F for 35 min. or until heated through. Top with remaining cheese; continue as directed.

Easy Chicken & Broccoli Alfredo

PREP: 10 min. **TOTAL:** 22 min.

- ½ **lb. fettuccine or spaghetti, uncooked**
- 2 **cups fresh broccoli florets**
- ¼ **cup KRAFT Zesty Italian Dressing**
- 1 **lb. boneless, skinless chicken breasts, cut into bite-size pieces**
- 1⅔ **cups milk**
- 4 **oz. (½ of 8-oz. pkg.) PHILADELPHIA Cream Cheese, cubed**
- ¼ **cup KRAFT Grated Parmesan Cheese**
- ½ **tsp. dried basil leaves**

COOK pasta as directed on package, adding broccoli for the last 2 min.

MEANWHILE, heat dressing in large nonstick skillet on medium-high heat. Add chicken; cook and stir 5 min. or until cooked through. Stir in milk, cream cheese, Parmesan cheese and basil. Bring to boil, stirring constantly. Cook 2 min. or until heated through.

DRAIN pasta mixture; return to pan. Add chicken mixture; mix lightly.

Makes 4 servings, 2 cups each.

Substitute: Substitute frozen peas, chopped red bell peppers or any of your favorite vegetables for the broccoli.

Creamy Pasta Primavera

PREP: 15 min. **TOTAL:** 30 min.

- 3 cups penne pasta, uncooked
- 2 Tbsp. **KRAFT** Light Zesty Italian Dressing
- 1½ lb. boneless, skinless chicken breasts, cut into bite-size pieces
- 2 zucchini, cut into chunks
- 1½ cups cut-up fresh asparagus (1 inch lengths)
- 1 red bell pepper, chopped
- 1 cup fat-free reduced-sodium chicken broth
- 4 oz. (½ of 8-oz. pkg.) **PHILADELPHIA** Neufchâtel Cheese, cubed
- ¼ cup **KRAFT** Grated Parmesan Cheese

COOK pasta in large saucepan as directed on package.

MEANWHILE, heat dressing in large skillet on medium heat. Add chicken and vegetables; cook 10 to 12 min. or until chicken is cooked through, stirring frequently. Add broth and Neufchâtel cheese; cook 1 min. or until cheese is melted, stirring constantly. Stir in Parmesan cheese.

DRAIN pasta; return to pan. Add chicken and vegetable mixture; toss lightly. Cook 1 min. or until heated through. (Sauce will thicken upon standing.)

Makes 6 servings, 1⅓ cups each.

Special Extra: Sprinkle with 2 Tbsp. chopped fresh chives or basil.

Substitute: Prepare using whatever vegetables you have on hand.

ENTRÉES

Easy Baked Parmesan Meatballs

PREP: 15 min. **TOTAL:** 40 min.

- **1 lb. ground beef**
- **½ cup KRAFT Grated Parmesan Cheese**
- **¼ cup chopped fresh parsley**
- **1 egg, beaten**
- **1 clove garlic, minced**

HEAT oven to 375°F. Mix ingredients; shape into 12 meatballs.

PLACE in foil-lined 15×10×1-inch baking pan.

BAKE 25 min. or until cooked through.

Makes 6 servings, 2 meatballs each.

Serving Suggestion: Try serving with your favorite hot cooked pasta and sauce and a quick bagged salad tossed with your favorite **KRAFT** Dressing, such as House Italian.

Substitute: Substitute 1 Tbsp. parsley flakes for the chopped fresh parsley.

Chicken and Spinach Risotto

PREP: 10 min. **TOTAL:** 30 min.

- **1 lb. boneless, skinless chicken breasts, cut into bite-size pieces**
- **1 Tbsp. oil**
- **4 cups baby spinach leaves, cleaned**
- **1½ cups instant white rice, uncooked**
- **1 cup grape or cherry tomatoes**
- **1 can (10½ oz.) condensed chicken broth**
- **½ cup water**
- **¼ cup KRAFT Grated Parmesan Cheese**

COOK chicken in hot oil in large deep nonstick skillet on medium heat 10 min. or until cooked through, stirring frequently.

ADD spinach, rice, tomatoes, broth and water; mix well. Bring to boil. Reduce heat to low; cover. Simmer 5 min., stirring occasionally.

STIR in cheese.

Makes 4 servings.

Substitute: Substitute dry white wine for ½ cup broth. Cover and refrigerate remaining broth for another use.

Substitute: Prepare using **KRAFT** Grated Three Cheese Blend.

Chicken-Parmesan Bundles

PREP: 35 min. **TOTAL:** 1 hour 5 min.

4 oz. (½ of 8-oz. pkg.) **PHILADELPHIA** Cream Cheese, softened

1 pkg. (10 oz.) frozen chopped spinach, thawed, well drained

1¼ cups **KRAFT** Shredded Low-Moisture Part-Skim Mozzarella Cheese, divided

6 Tbsp. **KRAFT** Grated Parmesan Cheese, divided

6 small boneless, skinless chicken breast halves (1½ lb.), pounded to ¼-inch thickness

1 egg

10 **RITZ** Crackers, crushed

1½ cups spaghetti sauce, heated

HEAT oven to 375°F. Mix cream cheese, spinach, 1 cup mozzarella cheese and 3 Tbsp. Parmesan cheese; spread onto chicken. Roll up tightly, starting at short ends. Secure with toothpicks, if desired.

BEAT egg in pie plate. Mix remaining Parmesan cheese and cracker crumbs in separate pie plate. Dip chicken in egg then in crumb mixture, turning to evenly coat both sides of each breast. Place, seam-sides down, in 13×9-inch baking dish sprayed with cooking spray.

BAKE 30 min. or until chicken is cooked through (165°F). Remove and discard toothpicks, if using. Top with spaghetti sauce and remaining mozzarella cheese.

Makes 6 servings.

Make Ahead: Assemble chicken bundles and place in baking dish as directed; refrigerate up to 4 hours. When ready to serve, bake at 375°F for 35 min. or until chicken is cooked through (165°F).

Special Extra: Stir chopped fresh basil and/or sliced black olives into spaghetti sauce before heating.

Foil-Wrapped Fish with Creamy Parmesan Sauce

PREP: 10 min. **TOTAL:** 22 min.

- **4 orange roughy fillets (1 lb.), thawed if frozen**
- **¼ cup KRAFT Mayonnaise**
- **¼ cup KRAFT Grated Parmesan Cheese**
- **⅛ tsp. ground red pepper (cayenne)**
- **2 zucchini, sliced**
- **½ of a red bell pepper, cut into strips**

HEAT grill to medium-high. Spray 4 (18×12-inch) sheets of heavy-duty foil with cooking spray; place 1 fillet in center of each. Spread with mayo; top with cheese, ground pepper and vegetables.

BRING up foil sides. Double fold top and ends to seal each packet, leaving room for heat circulation inside. Place on grill rack; cover grill with lid.

GRILL 10 to 12 min. or until fish flakes easily with fork.

Makes 4 servings.

Special Extra: Garnish each serving with lemon wedges.

Use Your Oven: Heat oven to 450°F. Assemble foil packets as directed; place on baking sheet. Bake 18 to 22 min. or until fish flakes easily with fork.

Parmesan Baked Salmon

PREP: 10 min. **TOTAL:** 25 min.

- ¼ cup **KRAFT** Mayonnaise
- 2 Tbsp. **KRAFT** Grated Parmesan Cheese
- ⅛ tsp. ground red pepper (cayenne)
- 4 salmon fillets (1 lb.), skin removed
- 2 tsp. lemon juice
- 10 **RITZ** Crackers, crushed

HEAT oven to 400°F. Mix mayo, cheese and pepper.

PLACE fish in foil-lined baking pan; top with lemon juice, mayo mixture and crumbs.

BAKE 12 to 15 min. or until fish flakes easily with fork.

Makes 4 servings.

Special Extra: Add ¼ tsp. dill weed to the mayo mixture before spreading onto fish.

Serving Suggestion: Serve with your favorite green vegetables, such as fresh green beans.

Easy Parmesan-Garlic Chicken

PREP: 5 min. **TOTAL:** 30 min.

- ½ cup **KRAFT** Grated Parmesan Cheese
- 1 env. **GOOD SEASONS** Italian Salad Dressing & Recipe Mix
- ½ tsp. garlic powder
- 6 boneless, skinless chicken breast halves (2 lb.)

HEAT oven to 400°F. Mix cheese, dressing mix and garlic powder.

MOISTEN chicken with water; coat with cheese mixture. Place in single layer in shallow baking dish.

BAKE 20 to 25 min. or until chicken is cooked through (165°F).

Makes 6 servings, 1 chicken breast each.

Special Extra: For a golden appearance after chicken is cooked through, set oven to Broil. Place 6 inches from heat source. Broil 2 to 4 min. or until chicken is golden brown.

Serving Suggestion: Serve with mixed green salad, tossed with your favorite **KRAFT** Dressing.

Parmesan-Crusted Chicken in Cream Sauce

PREP: 15 min. **TOTAL:** 30 min.

- 2 **cups instant brown rice, uncooked**
- 1 **can (14 oz.) fat-free reduced-sodium chicken broth, divided**
- 6 **RITZ Crackers, finely crushed**
- 2 **Tbsp. KRAFT Grated Parmesan Cheese**
- 4 **small boneless, skinless chicken breast halves (1 lb.)**
- 2 **tsp. oil**
- ⅓ **cup PHILADELPHIA Chive & Onion Light Cream Cheese Spread**
- ¾ **lb. asparagus spears, trimmed, steamed**

COOK rice as directed on package, using 1¼ cups broth and ½ cup water. Meanwhile, mix cracker crumbs and Parmesan cheese on plate. Moisten chicken with water, shaking off excess; coat both sides with crumb mixture. (Discard any remaining crumb mixture.)

HEAT oil in large nonstick skillet on medium heat. Add chicken; cook 5 to 6 min. on each side or until golden brown and cooked through (165°F). Place on serving plate; cover to keep warm.

ADD remaining broth and cream cheese spread to skillet. Bring just to boil, stirring constantly; simmer 3 min. or until thickened, stirring frequently. Spoon over chicken. Serve with rice and asparagus.

Makes 4 servings.

Variation: Prepare using **PHILADELPHIA** Light Cream Cheese Spread and stirring in 1 Tbsp. chopped fresh chives with the cream cheese spread.

Storing Asparagus: To store asparagus, stand fresh spears upright in a container filled with about 1 inch of water. Cover loosely with a plastic bag and refrigerate. Or, store in refrigerator with a damp paper towel wrapped around base of stalks and cover loosely with a plastic bag. Asparagus is best when cooked the day it is purchased, but will keep up to 3 or 4 days. Wash just before using.

Cheese & Chicken Fajita Quesadillas

PREP: 15 min. **TOTAL:** 32 min.

- ½ **lb. boneless, skinless chicken breasts, cut into thin strips**
- ¾ **cup each: sliced onions and red pepper strips**
- ½ **cup salsa**
- ½ **cup drained canned black beans, rinsed**
- 6 **flour tortillas (6 inch)**
- 1½ **cups KRAFT 2% Milk Shredded Sharp Cheddar Cheese**

COOK chicken in large skillet sprayed with cooking spray on medium-high heat 5 min., stirring frequently.

ADD onions and peppers; cook 4 to 5 min. or until crisp-tender. Stir in salsa and beans; cook 3 min. or until heated through, stirring occasionally.

TOP tortillas with chicken mixture and cheese; fold in half. Spray second large skillet with cooking spray. Heat on medium heat. Add quesadillas, in batches; cook 2 min. on each side or until evenly browned. Cut in half to serve.

Makes 6 servings, 1 quesadilla each.

Variation: Prepare as directed, substituting ½ cup drained canned corn for the black beans. Serve topped with shredded romaine lettuce, chopped fresh tomatoes and chopped cilantro.

Special Extra: Top each serving with 1 Tbsp. **BREAKSTONE'S** Reduced Fat or **KNUDSEN** Light Sour Cream.

Note: If you have only 1 large skillet, cook chicken mixture in skillet as directed, then transfer to bowl; cover to keep warm. Wipe out skillet, then spray with additional cooking spray and use to cook quesadillas as directed.